In The Wild

Siberian Tigers

Stephanie St. Pierre

Heinemann Library
Chicago, Illinois

Customer Service 888-454-2279

Visit our website at www.heinemannlibrary.com

Designed by Depke Design
Printed in Hong Kong

05 04 03 02 01
10 9 8 7 6 5 4 3 2

Library of Congress Cataloging-in-Publication Data
Cataloging-in-Publication data is on file at the Library of Congress.

Acknowledgments
The author and publishers are grateful to the following for permission to reproduce copyright material:
W. Perry Conway/Corbis, pp. 4 (far left), 6, 11, 22; Tom Brakefield/Corbis, pp. 4 (center), 9; Kennan Ward/Corbis, p. 4 (far right), 8; Lowell Georgia/Corbis, p. 5; Michele Burgess/Stock, Boston Inc./ PictureQuest, p. 7; Joe McDonald/Corbis, pp. 10, 18; Tom Brakefield, pp. 12, 13; Dr. Maurice Hornocker, p. 14; Bruce Coleman/Bruce Coleman Inc./PictureQuest, p. 15; Rod Williams/Bruce Coleman Inc./PictureQuest, p. 16; Byrn Colton/Corbis, p. 17; Dr. Maurice Hornocker/National Geographic Society, pp. 19, 20; Justine Pickett/Corbis, p. 21; Michael K. Nichols/National Geographic Society, p. 23.

Cover photograph: Tom Brakefield/Corbis

Some words are shown in bold, **like this.** You can find out what they mean by looking in the glossary.

Contents

Siberian Tiger Relatives 4

Where Siberian Tigers Live . . .6

The Family 8

Swimming 10

Hunting 12

Eating 14

Babies 16

Growing Up 18

Danger 20

Siberian Tiger Facts 22

Glossary 24

More Books to Read. 24

Index. 24

Siberian Tiger Relatives

The Siberian tiger is the largest of all cats. It is also called the Amur tiger. Its tiger relatives are the Bengal tiger and the Sumatran tiger.

bengal tiger

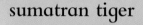
sumatran tiger

house cat

All tigers are members of the cat family, or **felines.** Tigers, lions, leopards, and jaguars are called big cats. They are all very much alike.

Where Siberian Tigers Live

Siberian tigers live in cold, mountainous areas in China and Russia. They like **woodlands.** They do not like **grasslands.**

Because they live in cold places, Siberian tigers have thicker, longer fur than other tigers. In winter their coats get even thicker and shaggier.

The Family

Adult **male** tigers live alone. **Female** tigers live with their babies. All Siberian tigers have yellow fur with brown stripes, but every tiger's stripes are **unique.**

Tigers have white fur on their bellies. They have long striped tails. By wagging and twitching their tails, tigers **communicate** with each other. A tail twitching quickly says, "Watch out!"

Swimming

Tigers like to be near water. They are good swimmers. Most tigers like to swim a lot, but Siberian tigers do not always swim.

Siberian tigers only swim in the summer.
They will swim to cool off on a hot day.
In the winter it is too cold to swim.

Hunting

Tigers hunt alone and do most of their hunting at night. They are **nocturnal** animals. Tigers can see much better at night than people can.

The tiger uses good eyesight and hearing to find **prey.** The tiger follows its prey until it is close enough to **pounce.** Once the prey has been caught, the tiger bites its neck to kill it quickly.

Eating

Tigers eat wild boar, deer, elk, fish, hare, and **livestock.** After it makes a **kill,** the tiger drags its food to a hiding place.

The tiger eats and rests and eats again until its food is all gone. It drinks lots of water while eating. The tiger may not eat again for three or four days.

Babies

Tiger mothers usually have two to four babies at a time. One of the cubs dies in almost every **litter.** At birth tiger cubs are totally blind and are very tiny.

Females must keep **male** tigers away so they won't kill the cubs. Tiger cubs stay with their mother between one and three years, until she has a new litter.

Growing Up

Young tigers make their own **kills** at about one and a half years old. They must find their own **home range** when they leave their mother.

Male tigers may go far away from their mothers, but **females** often stay close to them. Tigers scratch trees to tell other tigers where their home range begins and ends.

Danger

The tiger does not have any animal enemies. Its only enemy is human beings. Tigers are hunted for their meat, bones, and fur.

The Siberian tiger has been hunted so much that there are only a few hundred left in the wild. Most Siberian tigers live in zoos.

Siberian Tiger Facts

- Tigers have a loud strong roar but they cannot purr.

- Tiger paw prints are called pug marks.

• Siberian tigers have fewer stripes than other tigers.

• A group of tigers, usually a mother and cubs, traveling together is called a streak.

Glossary

camouflage pattern or color that helps an animal hide easily
communicate to make an idea or feeling understood
feline family of animals that includes all kinds of cats
female girl or woman
grassland area with few trees, but lots of long grass
groom to clean and smooth fur
home range area of land a big cat lives on
litter group of babies born together at the same time
littermates cubs born together in the same litter
male boy or man
nocturnal awake and active at night
prey animals hunted for food
stalk to watch and carefully follow
unique different in a special way

Index

babies 8, 16–17
cats 4, 5
cold 6, 7, 11
danger 20–21
eating 14–15
fur 7, 8, 9, 23

home range 18, 19
hunting 12–13, 14, 18, 20, 21
roaring 22
size 4
swimming 10–11

More Books to Read

Cooper, Jason. *The Siberian Tiger*. Vero Beach, Fla.: Rourke Book Co., 1997.

Dutemple, Lesley A. *Tigers*. Minneapolis, Minn.: Lerner Publications Co., 1996.

Welsbacher, Anne. *Tigers*. Minneapolis, Minn.: Abdo Publishing, 2000.